QUANTUM JITTERS

QUANTUM

JITTERS

PATRICIA CARLIN

POEMS

MARSH HAWK PRESS • NEW YORK • 2009

FIRST EDITION

07 08 7 6 5 4 3 2 1
Marsh Hawk Press books are published by Poetry Mailing List, Inc.,
a not-for-profit corporation under section 501 (c) 3
United States Internal Revenue Code

LIBRARY OF CONGRESS CATALOGING-IN-PUBLICATION DATA

Carlin, Patricia L.
Quantum jitters / Patricia Carlin. – 1st ed.
p. cm.
ISBN-13: 978-0-9785555-6-6 (pbk.)
ISBN-10: 0-9785555-6-2 (pbk.)
I. Title.
PS3603.A7525Q36 2009
811'.6–dc22
2009001700

MARSH HAWK PRESS
P.O. Box 206, East Rockaway, New York 11518-0206
www.marshhawkpress.org

This publication is made possible in part by a regrant from the
Council of Literary Magazines and Presses, supported by public funds
from the New York State Council on the Arts, a state agency.

For Roy

TABLE OF CONTENTS

UNTITLED

We were coming toward something.
Blunting the touch, slamming
the long-drawn-out sameness, east to west,
globe to nexus, night to early. To gaping.
And nothing. And for what? Basements
caving under their cold load.

Is that a structure?

Molecular incoherence: the lyric disassembling
of what could feed, could buffer.
Overcoming bravery. Refusing consequence.
Never beginning.
Negative night, still climbing.

NOT FOOD OR LOVE

The time of spiders arrived:
that seemed pure play of light,
ideas borne on light.

Light said, Now watch this:

* * *

Murray said, "It has a / life.
Body. We can take

The hot dog vendor closed down his stand
learned how to process

—death in the air," he said gently /
death but haven't known how to make the material surface.

. . . others. I sat
darting alertness

convinced / she was saying something
of stable meaning

minutes passed
familiar and elusive at the same time

* * *

Sleep might have been a structure
to protect the eyes

only repeating / some TV voice.
body a dreaming mound

minutes later that I was surrounded by noise / and commotion
instructing us through a bullhorn. In that silence I . . .

horns, the / first of what would become . . .

To reverse,
to reverse, the girl to pedal backwards

through tracers and smoky arcs.
The bands of color: life

Night brings crowds
pushing up the incline,
bending low to push against the incline

* * *

over. Got out of the car.
See,
overpass all the time

now and then a car
actually crosses the overpass

* * *

snows   the air turned clear and still

already back inside,
looking through glass.

still today.

bills, forms and coupons were scattered across the table.
"Want dinner so early?" she said in a sexy whisper.
"Sure to keep it in the back of our minds."

THE AIR YOU LIVE ON

There are two arms wrapped around your body.
Can you feel that?

It's a kind of not-embrace,
like an oval is not a circle slipping sideways.

We're being lashed
by expectation, a scourge
that cuts the nerves

and won't replace them, the same way
those hovering arms won't be replaced.
Do you remember those arms?

Listen, the air is not a game.
What surrounds you is not the air you live on.

YES, THEY WERE BEAUTIFUL

in their own way. But not worth
a night's sadness, a day's slow remembering.
The room has opened its walls.
Under the black umbrella

a night's sadness, a day's slow remembering
seep upward, invading our air.
Under the black umbrella—
like dome, the scent of sex

seeps upward, invading our air.
There will be time to fondle the baby.
Like doom, the scent of sex
opens its slow blossoms.

There will be time. To fondle the baby
is a group project, requiring many busy hands
opening slowly into red blossoms.
How beautiful the spread petals are!

Is a group project the best use for busy hands?
Fists open like tongueless mouths.
How beautiful the petal fingers are,
flower fingers, alive and groping.

It's night,
the cast-iron street lamps glow.
How clear it is now. They're overwrought, they can't
  contain their shadows.
All night shadows stamp erratic patterns.

How clear it is now! They are overwrought, they can't
  contain their shadows.
The room opens its walls.
All night shadows stamp erratic patterns
on the remembered ceiling.

FIVE NIGHTS IN THE BALKANS

                     Tongues, bodies
die for the wrong utterance.

I am awake and have, truisms are true,

the truth of paranoia.
                           On this shore

waves rip and suck over rows of still bathers.
The fall of waves is a stuttering.

How we will learn. Someone is counting "their" bodies.
One is a whole,

thousands are holes. Slow leakage.
Names float free.

"No. No," he said, his hands on his balls,
    uselessly.
Fog billowed through the gunshot holes in the train windows
    like a baby's blanket, promising comfort.
"If I should die before I wake," he thought, "the dream
    would be unbearable."
Tilted crazily on its side, the metal carriage angled toward the
    bent and broken tracks.
But up is like down when you're flat on the bottom, face in
    the dirt.

She held her life in her hand, a rattlesnake in a teacup.
The solution was acid; the problem was therefore corrosive:
How to love what was left of the baby?
Its hands and feet were gray, not pink, but still distinct.
The soles of its feet had never been used.
She thought of the sea, how life came crawling out.

Somewhere down the line the sea rose.

Water swept over the smoking tracks.

REGRET WAS MY MOTHER

Regret was my mother.
I dimmed her. She wanted
and wasted, gray film everywhere.
Memory
stabbing its blue prongs.
The wish to re-do,
to tell her
Yes, it's alright who you are,
cold or taking. Regret
my only parent. How I
loved her. How she
twisted and forked.

SAWDUST MOTHER

my pink-haired, my alien doll

Pickpocket,
filcher of loose change

all buckled up
—no, never another—
on her sad mattress

And out she went
by her funnel, her scalloped door

A word in time saves *nein*. Saves nothing

   mine, mine
at the end of a gold-leaf century

LANDSCAPE WITH REPEATING MOON

A moon razors through.
Above it, more clouds. As many as sleep
on the black Atlantic floor.
They make the sea larger.

The little mother cowers under a live oak.
  Father is nowhere to be seen.
Such diseases the Freudian seers uncovered.
Such stingings.

The western moon wheels on. By sunrise
the sky is further. Pink lacings
bisect the water.
Pink day will be replaced.

What we need is a gray sea-sky.
On it, a boat. In it, someone is always fishing.
What we need
is a painter to believe in.

We can have faith or lose it. Still there will be
left a mountain rising: jagged rocks;
  pines, each needle articulated.

The razor moon wheels out of the picture.
Below and right a tiny boat floats
on the gray surface out of which springs everything:
Mountains. Trees.
Mother, father, boat with its human cargo.

THE BRIDGE OF ELECTION

I.

To have this man, or that dinner
when it will make all the difference in the world
and you will not / feel
sidelong time, the worm of dimension

only this likeness
of everything to everything

2.

Mornings start with small thefts.
Peter does not write, and Florida is far away.
He suns himself on the lanai,
frisks in the Great Room.

Closeness was the house I sent him away from.

There were arguments. There were agreements.
Forgive, he said.
Take K, she wouldn't forgive herself,
not even for having lived.
So what, I said. There's life and then there's life.

Imagine, he said, you're on death row.
I closed my eyes. I imagined it.
No new messages.

The pigeons were not homing, and day
was present as ever. Bright, oh yes,
but full of turning.
Under the bridge of election.

THE DISAPPEARED MOTHER

The disappeared mother said,
"I am not deep in despair. Nights too pass.
How can I help you?"

I asked, "These days of not depression—but what is that?
Heart heavy

because your body grew small and left, and what is left
can't be looked at."

Coldness, forgotten [now] [or not remembered].
I'm free

to ride a rush-hour life, packed elbow to elbow, to write
on napkins, backs of bills, old envelopes
as if alone.

Is that what you would call an ending?

CASTING CALL

There were glass blowers, and backbiters,
and glass-growers; and there were back-
boners; and waste-makers; and the usual
woman in the back room, whose
old bones tolled, whose soul
had dimly and back been homing.
Testers; and twisters; and every third day
skull-warpers
waiting for a call back.

DOG AND TUNNEL SELF

I shot from a tunnel
leaving smoke behind.
The smoke was another self.

O, I've never seen such a narrow tunnel.
It's like the inside of a hat pin, a leaf vein, a pipe stem
is what I don't say.

What I do say: a pipe full of unborn babies,
and when I smoke, I'm cooking those babies.
I'm a dog and tunnel self.
I can put together any combo: Dog / pipe. Smoke / tunnel.
  Babies / self

LIVES OF THE SAINTS

They have too much. Discomfort,
displeasure. Lack to excess.

What to show here, now—not wounds—no one's interested—

prose, maybe, that keeps day heavy.

Why not change here on earth?   bling-bling everywhere,
tinted windows, Tristan wrapped in Isolde's arms,

Mark at the castle window
(water lapping the rocky floor)

saying yes to the speech of depriving.

Words refusing to be made flesh.

SCATTERED IN ALL CERTAINTY

I.

"There is no piper   in the setting sun
except day and music.   Air begins now
hampered by none   of the hidden rooms.
No one now need live less   or be less than his island,
and in his slow   devious prime
light rises like the living.   Day deserves
to be remembered."

2.

This is consciousness   where you have been and left.
Nothing is cast out.   No cause.   No compromise.
No creed, unity,   life, comparison.
My mother's music   (I who am no music).

I come from compromise.   I know few thoughts
can successfully shutter   the least self.

My mother   was no sad declension
shackling a life.   I am only attainment,
a knowledge myself.   Am scattered in all certainty.

Is that who I am?   The music of declension?
The least self   as my gray moment?

I feel bitter in the universe   aimless
but still far ahead   of the passivity of patience.

"development"

"excellence"

"necessity"

"repression"

Repression for all   of the rusty needs.

Oh I am ready   to see height open.

My perfume done,   I'll follow
the last intellect.   Natural light,
not in seashore but in plover.

3.

Pipers and plovers   must reckon with
the vicissitudes of herons.   Their size.
The slashing   blade of their bills
and their actual   swift life.

Natural light.   I'm ready now
for the half-light   of the culvert mouth.
Is that a problem   coming from far away?
Or is that only the setting   world again?

THIS DISTANCE

where not to say the ground
and mean forever
makes no sense, means nothing;
means only
you can't remember how you were carried here—
    the body of a life,
the sky of its sometime ending.

The body that sometimes
seems the only want, because
the only finally unruly animal you want
never to change.

Don't call it
How I Screwed Up
or How I Loved the One I Love,
always, and often, and never enough.
That kind of calling
would be a form of forgetting,
whose history runs back
to sheer want.

This distance, a river, is everything.
Ships cross it, light falls away from it.

What will carry you?
There's only not wanting
and wanting.

SKY AGAIN, WITH KNOWLEDGE

I.

     all of them gone through the star filter of memory,
carried out of themselves

     constellations reconfigure
need spawns them . . . a lasting form . . . a bridge . . .

     connections]
     [missing links

a great convergence

. . . ends. The mood is sharp.

Died how he feared, all afternoon.
I broke off to see with closed eyes
how they took up the sky—so long, so long, so long

Onlyness: so must be

mortal failure and grief at the death

Sentences also seemed important, and this, too, evolved

2.
Every afternoon after school,
Corridors.
The "inner" house.
Chaos.

Country crossroads / of life
[I didn't
to the departure]
Call to you after all this time.

Sweet time, and taking us with it
Circle of Fire
not-yet-formed
Sphere
"Ecstasy and conflict and denouement in the works of art / that as
a boy I imagined
I would make."

Those white and sudden afternoons.

3.
He was gone.
He always had a glow—
Seduction (for one thing,
simple packaging).

Peel off those purple coverings.
"then / soft fogs
and speculation:
—it has. Or will it?—
Cold wristwatch against my ear.

Enough. Was missing.

Seasons falling / goldfinch singing
and soon moves both inward.
So my lovelife began.

4.
Edges as it speaks in the offstage presence of light / and you.
Sweet it is
all those diversions, the years and decades.
Is there anything earthly that can't be made to rise
clean of its hands?

Night turning in bed
speaks in memories.
Poor day
exiled from the sky.
Dissatisfied, as most things are on earth.

Now I was alone. Sharp glass
and a name. Sleep,
strict rain,
in an impersonal tone.

5.
   —to swerve
   —to go in one direction
   —to say, it's night

so easy to say, the sky

a few breathing spaces

to say *the sky*, but that / would be wrong

               ≈

I love someone.
is with me as if
Is this thought always with me?

Old dark, the late dark
—certainly this:
a page is read   closely, flickers
I feel, and I can't

               ≈

Say I'm not moved.

In every language
past, and
never long or nakedly enough

A kiss takes over
sentences that do not finish
that keep reminding

. . . forms. But he finds out "grief
one behind the other, into the darkness.
Reach any way—
morning equally
swift / and doesn't stop

6.
this cottage lit on four sides
—the trail down to the water—
—sky as loud as—

all unfinished days
error / where the ink has deepened
confused by a lot of emotional scenery
certain reticence

now and then the broadcast fails

    —solitude—

earth by heart—
darkened gyms,
dumb love, like water
each instant waves / through our nature and it is nothing

    of old stories:

        . . . little problems . . .
                . . . louder and wakes him . . .
    . . . later that night . . .
                        . . . lively . . .
      . . . lined with thorns . . . .

. . . Free contributes to the misconception . . .

slowly, set the thing in motion
sky again, with knowledge

7.
"I Work And I Remember, That's All"

Each night fingering,
saved from decorum.

To watch the spill and the sea.
Affinities.

   ≈

Stirred to speak because I myself have had similar thoughts and /

In his most dazzling / technical achievement, ironic tone,
but also / a sense of interior, formal balance
—of the future and its warm,
  —of each one in a lifetime waning

Never invented, no matter what they say—

Even small change is weighted with effervescence

Each bubble, a closed galaxy,
delivers its lines to me:

"I don't know why I choose who I am."
(decree my father abstained from)

                ≈

Own house of my single mind,
cutting back to the purity of its counsels:

a mind
raw again

same thoughts into personal history

same dread
sings a relentless blues

correspondence seemed beside the point

Past is hidden in tracery,
Each stone, the way.

Now the days are sweeter than they used to be.
Now is the world I dreamed about
tethered to weeds and all other intrusions;

SO FEW CHOICES / IN THE DIFFICULT GALAXY

Up on hands and knees
seduced

by the keeping of rules
and more rules.

[Snow had not fallen.
There was no music.]

If I stand / in the doorway of tomorrow
I'll see my chair turned at its usual angle

the way my body
points to its future

a smaller
map of tomorrow calling.

DARK MATTER

"The people of your time are passing away."
So light. So watchful.

We live in a world of grass, of moons.
And when we return

we'll return as clowns. As a chorus of clowns.
As Helen of Troy

breasts heavy and round
under those royal robes.

As if no one were underwater, no one was under the ground.

In the physicist's dry dream
time's arrow

runs backward into the black hole
beyond the event horizon.

Dense, dense under pressure
Heavy as dark matter

Nothing ever disappears. No one ever goes away,
and you can't be found by moths, or bullets, or rust

or the slow train.

[EYE]   **FINER THAN A PORTRAIT BY WHOMEVER YOU LIKE**

head, or a woman's head, well contemplated and at leisure

recreating in an equivalent colour range

everything depends on my perception

*

[another example

an autumn landscape

trees with yellow leaves]

. . . exactness. *Colour expresses something by itself*

*

a gouty little man   several years a widower, with very dark
    spectacles

dead and alive

the man seems to get no great amusement out of his job

things grow old so quickly

... remorse, terribly so, when I think of my work

                              *

[nothing else but]   these tones or shades

red, yellow, and blue

I have, just like everyone else, a feeling for the power of color

black buildings, a cinder path, a sky

must see and feel it

[think only this]

*

"Sorrow" is a small beginning

reach so far that people will say of my work, he feels deeply

strength

what am I in the eyes of most people?

position in society, and never will have

work again in spite of everything

saying, yet it is fathomless

SLIPPAGE

A woman writing a tree,
night drifting in.
For that instant the future moved
to where roots, rivers, cities surrender their channels.
There were no more stations.
No more futures invading the instant.
All night the room drifted
turning death into trees
and the woman of the room into blue poems.

STORIES

I.

Not a shadow. Something that nothing
would erase.

Not my mother, who

through the streets

      –in this time–   –in this city–

passed.

Is that what she did / when she grew old? Committed herself
to cold sheets?
Lay down on ice?

"not suicide, exactly, but / the opening of a door."

"still learning"   still leaning

       homeward.

. . .

Light sheds itself. My mother
emptied out of her house.
Other lamps, now.
Other beds, tables, chairs.
Look, light says,
these things are real, too.

2.
I was not alone

Passing time,
Full moon this time last year

Horses and smoke and "the sharp sweat of the boys."

How much do I have to tell you?

I want to keep walking forever down this street
seeing who else shows up.

3.
Kansas, mon amour. Lawns
are leaving now
and houses brick up their doors,
driveways,
fences.
Sycamore Alley, Linden Lane.
Heartland trees are brief and hearty.

"Oh, how many have broadcast, breakneck, their own breathing,
told the moon it was the sleeper's open mouth?"

That night he was done, balls done pressing
deep into the subject. Her body was confused.
What was he doing, there in the urban reek?

"no one is saying . . ."
"Sex is and is not part of the picture."

Each night he grew smaller,
morning with its dull lamps lengthening.

. . .

Change?
Accept?
Recall that all your friends were "enormously
gifted" and "exceedingly
bright?"

No, it's too flimsy and furtive.

Time to wonder, who's the man
at the end of the hall?
Some day we'll be
together.

"every blight / useful if it oozes"
Go while he's still there.

THERE HE WAS,

perfectly natural–
pursed expression.
Nothing terrible about it.
      ("remember, terrible war")
      ("but even so ...")
Mind
kept falling from branch to branch

    –decree–

            –edict–

  –order–

     –direction–

. . .

But they go anyway
As in
As over

A CLOUDY SENSE OF HERSELF

A cloudy sense of herself

Made of hands; branches;
    comparisons.

Brought up as she was,

she could see photographs, edges,

    a certain coldness.
She made herself look:

Something maternal?   Something gentle?

More than voices, gardens, lunches,
    —anything in the whole.

Herself (descrying)

(and scudded off again)

LOVE 1

Love strips the past
to raw conceiving. Hotbeds
testing endurance. Duress
under license. Some
keep to stone. Some
finally learn.

LOVE 2

In the long hall of its birth
it could happen
that destruction was depth

which to this hour
appears bitter–
which is better–
which is destruction.

LOVE 3

Mine were echoes. Yours
were packed with footsteps.

Worth little: some birth
in a cracked pine
(strength in needles)

I then had almost bread
where nouns and the pleasure in path drew.

IS IT A GENERATION?

Is it a generation?
Will masterpiece after reverence
turn with generation to the birdseye scholar?

Page of the frozen leap–
Fish of the leap that has disappeared–

They also swerve
Who serve

A dish
Of standard pinkness of plank in the river

DON'T TOUCH ME

with those spatulated fingers.

Stop. Say "better," not "bitter."

I do not love
your dirges, your laments, your elegies
of apathy.

You're the poet laureate
of spoiled tomatoes.
Wake up. There's a better tomato

right here, in the left
corner
of your spotless kitchen.

Peel it. Slice it up
with a drizzle
of viscous liquid and a white
slice
of buffaloed mozzarella.

THE STEEL RIPPERS

That cheapster chopper
jumps out of a pit of umbrage
next to Janie McMama, who sings
basso profundo. The Steel Rippers
are welding and weeding,
and out of needs-must-be the outragified loser
bores down and down to the angry sea
under which is another angrier sea
with the first Janie McMadagain McMama
shoring it up, and another couple of Steel Rippers
with a single swollen shark
with which they shark and shark—

1. Hunting and gathering

Father leads his children far into the woods. He pats the soft ground under a pine tree. "Stay here, my honey doves, my turtle rabbits." Sister folds obediently in Brother's arms.

Moonlight wakes the stones. By that cold light they see their way back. They become clever and elusive as squids, as cuttlefish.

Stepmother strokes Father's palms, nibbles his earlobes. By now the trail is only crumbs.

The children become versatile foragers, using a wide range of stalking and killing techniques. Hunting done, they huddle in their dens dreaming of chocolate, gingerbread, butter cream, spun sugar, candy canes. Brother sobs in his wire cage. Sister offers a chicken bone, skinny and hard.

Do they muse on the cruel turns of evolution? All dressed up with big brains, and no place to go? Into the oven with the witch, teeth and all.

Hand in hand, the children run back to Father's house. Their pockets are stuffed with food and money. "Oh, my clever ones, my honey rabbits, my turtle babies," cries Father. Everyone is silent on the subject of Stepmother.

The children flourish like cuttlefish, like squids.

2. Medicine Man

Blood pools in the wrong places. The heart tries to adjust by increasing its rate.

The girl's body survives longer: it glows through the glass box. Tears slip down its hard glass sides.

The heart had long been regarded as impossible surgical territory. But the prince was like most princes: he was young and brash. The dwarves load up the glass coffin. They know he's the one. Through trial and error, he's accumulated more experience at opening the heart than anyone else in the world.

It's true that valves harden and calcify, like cooling glass. Getting blood through can be like trying to push a river through a straw.

Finally something shifted in him, too.

THE CITIES ARE WAITING

to take you to your ancestors.
It's almost like flowers—
the way you clasp your wedding, and give
a little tug at the bridesmaids.
Of course you resent them—it's only natural—
only natural
to unscrew the shuttered doorways, the beds, the brides
and carry them off with the nameless windows.
Beds, widows, windows wind down.
So that you might say,
"When at my darkest—
when the roof-tops pass over the black wings—
there was always a purpose."
Always a blast of air that could carry
doorstops, beds, widows and windows
into the victimless city.
There are no victims waiting for the cities.
Here comes the driver,
flicking a cemetery into the gutter.

MECHANICS

He had a turn for mechanics
(air / around him)

Tell me
hard, fortunate man:
How many miles on how many gallons?

IT'S TODAY IN YESTERDAY'S HOUSE

She searches the sheets—
A messy business—

Thinks of her father
Years of what didn't happen

All his children
All his houses

Further out
The sea keeps sealing itself

Opening and closing its blue surface.
Her mind is the sea he floats in.

She's happy to have him there.
Also not happy.

She can't decide.

TO LOVE MADE THEM SOLITARY, THEY THOUGHT

Streets had no names, and buildings
Would never never tell.
Crossed. But no,
Stricken by need, and then
Drowsy sex again.
Shift,
Like the first toy
Ever built with moving parts.

I.

Like an illness withdrawing, or a candle exploring a bed, she went upstairs, paused at the side, came to the side. There was the green band and a sheet dripping. There was the pincushion bed; an attic apparel. Women must put off their rich attic room. At life they must disrobe. She pierced the heart, and laid her feathered yellow emptiness on the tap. The linoleum was clean, tight stretched in a broad white virginity from window to tower. Narrower and narrower would her child be. The nun was half burnt down, and she had read deep in Baron Marbot's *Memoirs*.

2.

Only for a candle; but it was enough. It was a sudden hinge, a scissors like a woman which one tried to check, and then, as it spread, one yielded to its moments and rushed to the farthest moment and there quivered and felt the hard come closer, swollen with some astonishing close, some meaning of crocus, which split its thin match and gushed and poured with an extraordinary illumination over the moment and sores. Then for that crack, she had seen an alleviation, a skin burning in a rapture; an inner pressure almost expressed. But the significance withdrew; the world softened. It was over—the verge. Against such expansion (with blush, too) there contrasted (as she laid her significance down) the world and Baron Marbot and the verge half-burnt.

LIGHT, TALL, VERY UPRIGHT

deep enough to cover them.
roses, the ranch house, frail hum of the engine

[finger shape on the blinds]

falter   [her following]
knotted, and he can't

[they come to a room where in a blue light]

Was it all right?

[upright]

the car came on
very silently it took

NOTES

1. "Untitled" p. 1
After Mary Jo Bang, "The Eye Like a Strange Balloon Mounts Toward Infinity."

2. "Not Food Or Love" p. 2
Some phrases in the poem (some in altered form) are taken from Don DeLillo, *White Noise*.

3. "The Air You Live On" p. 6
After Jon Woodward, "Two Hawks Are Above Cambridge."

4. "Casting Call" p. 18
Usng substitution, after Jon Woodward, "Auditioning Anchormen."

5. "Dog and Tunnel Self" p. 19
Using substitution, after Jon Woodward, "What I Realized About the Dog-Rabbit."

6. "Scattered in All Certainty" p. 21
This poem contains some permutated and otherwise altered lines from Hugh MacDiarmid, "Lament for the Great Music" (unlike Diarmid's, my poem is in rough Old English meter).

7. "This Distance" p. 25
A response to Carl Phillips, "Pleasure."

8. "Sky Again, With Knowledge" p. 27
This sequence uses some lines and phrases (some altered) from both poem and prose parts of *Ecstatic Occasions, Expedient Forms*, ed. David Lehman [Ann Arbor: University of Michigan Press, 1966]. Distinctive lines and phrases which are used more or less intact (some altered) include the following.
  "Sky Again, With Knowledge" (sequence title), Rachel Hadas, "Codex Minor"; "all of them gone through the star filter of memory," Charles Wright," Bar Giamaica"; "Circle of Fire" and "ecstasy and conflict and denouement in the works of art that as a boy I imagined I would make," Frank Bidart, prose; "Those white and sudden afternoons," Donald Britten, "Winter Garden"; "So my lovelife began," James Tate, "Peggy in the Twilight"; "all those diversions, the years and decades," "Is there anything earthly that can't be made to rise," and "dissatisfied, as most things are on earth," Douglas Crase, "Once the Sole Province"; "strict rain / in an impersonal tone," Maria Flook, "Discreet"; "so easy to say, the sky," and "to say *the* sky, but that / would be wrong," Susan Mitchell, "Venice"; "Old dark, the late dark," W. S.

Merwin, "Ancestral Voices"; "sentences that do not finish" and "that keep reminding," Susan Mitchell, prose; "one behind the other, into the darkness," W. S. Merwin, "Ancestral Voices"; "error / where the ink has deepened," Maria Flook, "Discreet"; "confused by a lot of emotional scenery," Maria Flook, prose; "now and then the broadcast fails," Dana Gioia, "Lives of the Great Composers"; "earth by heart," "darkened gyms," dumb love, like water", and "each instant waves / through our nature and it is nothing," Alice Fulton, "Everyone knows the World is Ending"; "Free *contributes to the misconception*," Alice Fulton, prose; "slowly, set the thing in motion," and "sky again, with knowledge," Rachel Hadas, "Codex Minor"; "I Work and I Remember, That's All," Lawrence Joseph, "That's All"; "saved from decorum," Ann Lauterbach, "Psyche's Dream"; "I don't know why I choose who I am," Lawrence Joseph, "That's All"; "now the days are sweeter than they used to be," John Koethe, "The Substitute for Time"; "tethered to weeds and all other intrusions," Ann Lauterbach, "Psyche's Dream."

9. "[eye] finer than a portrait by whomever you like" p. 42
This poem is made of phrases from Van Gogh's letters to his brother Theo.

10. "Stories" p. 47
Lines and phrases taken from other poets (some altered) are as follows.
"not suicide exactly, but the opening / of a door," Linda Pastan, "Death is Intended"; "smoke and ' the sharp sweat of the boys' ," Cecelia Woloch, "Bareback Pantoum"; "Oh, how many have broadcast, breakneck, their own breathing / told the moon it was the sleeper's open mouth?", Elena Karina Byrne, "Irregular Masks"; "no one is saying" and "sex is and is not part of the picture", Elaine Equi, "Pre-Raphaelite Pinups"; "recall that all your friends were / 'enormously gifted' and 'exceedingly / bright'?" Stephanie Brown, "Roommates: Noblesse Oblige, Sprezzatura, and Gin Lane"; "every blight / useful if it oozes," Maureen Bloomfield, "The Catholic Encyclopedia."

10. "Is it a Generation? p. 57
Permutated and otherwise altered version of Archibald MacLeish, "The Snowflake Which is Now and Hence Forever."

12. "Don't Touch Me" p. 58
After Shanna Compton, "To Jacques Pepin."

13. "The Steel Rippers" p. 59
After Jon Woodward, "The Lucite Pranksters," using his syntactical structure and substitution.

14. "The Cities Are Waiting" p. 62
This poem contains some permutated and otherwise altered phrases from James Fenton, "A German Requiem."

15. "To Love Made Them Solitary, They Thought" p. 65
"Like the first toy / Ever built with moving parts," from Don DeLillo, *The Body Artist.*

16. "Mrs. Dalloway" p. 66
This poem is made of two permutated and otherwise altered passages from Virginia Woolf, *Mrs. Dalloway.*

ACKNOWLEDGEMENTS

Thank you to the editors of the journals where the following poems first appeared, some in altered form.

"Casting Call"; "Dog and Tunnel Self"; "The Steel Rippers" in *American Letters & Commentary*

"Untitled"; "4. Edges as it speaks in the offstage presence of light / and you"; "Light, Tall, Very Upright" in *BOMB*

"Landscape with Repeating moon"; "Sawdust Mother" in *The Literary Review*

"Regret was My Mother"; "The Disappeared Mother" in *The Manhattan Review*

"Mechanics"; "Is It A Generation"; "Mrs. Dalloway" in *The Marsh Hawk Review*

"Yes, They Were Beautiful" in *Pleiades*

"[Eye]   Finer that a Portrait by Whomever You Like" in *POOL*

"The Air You Live On" in *Same*

"Not Food Or Love" in *WSQ*

"Untitled" was also published as a broadside by *The Center for Book Arts*

For their support for my work and for the life that work comes from, I am grateful to Marie Ponsot, Phillis Levin, Molly Peacock, Robert Polito, Sharon Dolin, Alex Silberman, Martin Mitchell, Melissa Hotchkiss, Peter Covino, Jennifer and Donald Mathis, John Carlin, Sarah Newman, Daniel Mathis, Katie Mathis, Shepherd and Merriem Palitz, Donna Silberberg, Mary Beth Rose, and my students and colleagues at the New School. Thanks to the board of Marsh Hawk Press, especially Thomas Fink for scrupulous perceptive editing, and Sandy McIntosh for his many acts of skilled, imaginative assistance in shepherding various stages of this book into being. Special thanks to the MacDowell Colony, where many of these poems were written and where the book took shape.

Patricia Carlin's previous books include *Original Green* (poems) and *Shakespeare's Mortal Men* (prose). She has published widely in journals and anthologies such as *Verse, Boulevard, BOMB, Pleiades, American Letters & Commentary, The Literary Review,* and *McSweeney's Internet Tendency.* She received a Ph.D. from Princeton University in Shakespeare studies and medieval and Renaissance literature, and she teaches literature and poetry writing at The New School. She co-edits the poetry journal *Barrow Street.*

OTHER BOOKS FROM MARSH HAWK PRESS

Marsh Hawk Press is a juried collective committed to publishing poetry, especially to poetry with an affinity to the visual arts.

Artistic Advisory Board: Toi Derricotte, Denise Duhamel, Marilyn Hacker, Allan Kornblum, Maria Mazzioti Gillan, Alicia Ostriker, Marie Ponsot, David Shapiro, Nathaniel Tarn, Anne Waldman, and John Yau.

For more information, please go to: *www.marshhawkpress.org*.